Rev. Barb:

Thanks for your love and
inspiration over the years!

God bless,
Rick Rennie

THE WAY OF
AUTHORITY AND POWER

Rick Rannie

CROSSBOOKS
PUBLISHING

CrossBooks™
A Division of LifeWay
1663 Liberty Drive
Bloomington, IN 47403
www.crossbooks.com
Phone: 1-866-879-0502

First published by CrossBooks 9/14/2011

ISBN: 978-1-4627-0643-3 (sc)

Library of Congress Control Number: 2011916373

Printed in the United States of America
This book is printed on acid-free paper.

*Any people depicted in stock imagery provided by Thinkstock are models,
and such images are being used for illustrative purposes only.*

Certain stock imagery © Thinkstock.

All Scripture references are from the King James Version of the Bible unless noted otherwise

Preface

The Lord said to me that we are on the precipice of a great healing movement. The mantra of the coming days will be "The Healing Jesus". If this is true then we as the church must be prepared to move in our inheritance of authority and power. How many have been frustrated by the fact that we have prayed and not seen results in praying for the sick? How many times have you cried out to God and said as the disciples, "Why could not we cast him out?"(Matthew 17:19).

This is a "how to" book on moving in the authority and power of God. God wants us to move in the fullness of His authority and power. Jesus was right when He said, "The works I do you shall do also." (John 14:12).

Acknowledgments

I thank my Lord and Savior Jesus Christ for helping me write this book. I could not have accomplished this book had it not been for my wife Patricia and my children: Nicole, Benita and Jeremy.

I thank God for the support of my parents, Richard A. and Dolores Rannie; my sister and her husband Kim and Mike DeGraphenreed; and all my family and friends.

To Pastor's Harold and Sherren McKenzie, and my Unity Church of Jesus Christ family, I appreciate your love, inspiration, support and prayers. To Joan Lisle, thank you for helping me edit this book.

To Pastor Dave Janseen, and the State College Christian and Missionary Alliance Church, thank you for letting me learn and work with your healing team.

To my grandmothers Martha Penn and Beryl Rannie who I loved dearly and died too young thank you.

To all the men and women of God who have inspired me: Rev. Ruth Benton, Rev. Robert Hargrove, Bishop Gerald Loyd, Margie Loyd, Bishop Sidney Wheatley, Dr. Haroon Kharem, Dr. Audrey Kharem, Pastor Melvin Jenkins, Rev. Barb Knight and the Whirlwind team,

Prophetess Debbie Botteicher, Prophetess Bonnie Pence, Prophet Dave Ross, and Pastor Ron Crawford, thank you.

To all that supported this book, thank you and God bless you.

Table of Contents

PART I –
The foundation of our authority and power

Chapter 1

INTRODUCTION

Herein is our love made perfect, that we may have boldness in the day of judgment: **because as He is, so are we in this world.** *I John 4:17*

The promise of the Word is that as Jesus is so are we in this world. If the Scripture says this it is true. We must then learn about Jesus so we can become like Him. The scripture says the following about Jesus in Ephesians 1: 20-22:

20.

Which He wrought in Christ, when He raised Him from the dead and set Him at His own right hand in the heavenly places.

21.

Far above all principality, and power, and might, and dominion and every name that is named not only in this world, but also in that which is to come.

22.

And hath put all things under His feet, and gave Him to be the head over all things to the church.

In Matthew 28:18, Jesus says, "All power is given unto me in heaven and in earth.

Daniel 7: 13-14 says about Jesus:

13.

I saw in the night visions, and, behold one like the Son of Man came to the Ancient of days, and they brought him near before Him.

14.

*And there was given Him **dominion**, and **glory**, and a **kingdom** that all people, nations, and languages, should serve Him: His dominion is an everlasting dominion, which shall not pass away, and His kingdom that which shall not be destroyed.*

By looking at these Scriptures we see that Jesus has all power and authority. When He died the power of resurrection came and raised Him from the dead. Jesus is now seated at the right hand of God in heavenly places far above all principality and power. Years before Jesus was born Daniel saw Jesus having dominion or authority, and a kingdom. He is the King of Kings and Lord of Lords. He has a name above all names, and every tongue will confess He is Lord to the glory of the Father (Philippians 2: 10-11).

Right now Jesus has all power and authority. The enemy has no power over Him. The question the church must ask is; do we walk in this same power and authority? Does not the Scripture say as He is so are we in this world? Did not Jesus say the works I do we will do also and greater (John 14:12)? Is the church supposed to walk in the same glory, dominion and kingdom as Jesus?

Daniel 7:27 says:

> And the **kingdom** and **dominion** and the greatness of the kingdom under the whole heaven, shall be given to **the people of the saints of the Most High**.

According to Daniel we are to walk in the authority and kingdom of our Lord Jesus. Paul says the following about our inheritance in Romans 8:17:

> And if children, then heirs; heirs of God, and joint-heirs with Christ, if so be that we suffer with Him, that we may be also glorified together.

This means whatever Jesus has is mine. Therefore we have a right to the same authority and power that Jesus has. The question still remains: How do we enter into this?

My personal experience

I remember when I was ten years old and my grandmother was sick with cancer. I knew Jesus was a healer and I prayed for her healing. My family sent letters to preachers with healing ministries to pray for her healing, but she was not healed. God's grace allowed me to still believe that He is a healer even though she died. Do not let death shake your faith in Him, because His Word is true. From that early time I desired to be used in the power of God but I did not have someone to teach me how to move in it. I remember seeking for His power and God told me it was in me. I received it but I did not see any results. As I look back to that time I realize that was the start of learning about the power of God. The Word says we will do greater works, but my question was how? That was a time of frustration for me.

Several years ago while I was at work a spirit of the enemy stood next to me and said, "You have no power over me." I tried to think of every Scripture I knew about the power of God to get that demon away from me. After a few minutes the spirit departed. I have to admit that I was a little shook up. After that experience I prayed and said Father cause me to know for myself and without a shadow of doubt that I have power over the enemy. A few days later God gave me an open vision of Ephesians 1:21, and 2:6. He showed me that not only is He seated far above all principality and power, and might, and dominion, but we are too. I saw the enemy under my feet. He also showed me Ephesians 2: 5-6:

5.

Even when we were dead in sins, hath quickened us together with Christ, (by grace ye are saved);

6.

And hath raised us up together, and made us sit together in heavenly places in Christ Jesus.

This means that we have also been risen up together to sit with Christ in heavenly places. This means we have authority over all the power and authority of the enemy. I had heard these scriptures preached but it was God who made it real to me that day. From that day I knew the enemy was under my authority because of what Jesus did at the cross. Every doctrine of the church must have the cross as its foundation or else it is not true. Because of the cross we have a right to authority and power.

As a church how do we come to the point where we all can say as He is so are we in this world? How do we get to the point where as He is in power, and authority, so are we in this earth? Daniel said, "The kingdom and dominion will be given to the saints of the Most High." If we are going to be like Jesus we need to see how He moved in power and authority. We know the kingdom and authority is ours, because Ephesians 2: 5-6 says, "By grace we are saved and we are made to sit in heavenly places far above all principality and power." We must learn how to receive this part of our inheritance. We need to ask God to make this Scripture real, and then we will have a release of power and authority in the church.

Chapter 2

THE CROSS LEADS TO POWER

5.

> *Even when we were dead in sins, hath quickened us together with Christ, (By grace ye are saved);*

6.

> *And hath raised us up together, and made us sit together in heavenly places in Christ Jesus. Ephesians 2: 5-6*

As we see from the above passage, when we are saved we are placed in Christ Jesus in heavenly places far above all principality and power. We have authority over the enemy. The way is made for us to be in Christ Jesus by the cross. To be in Him means to come into an abiding relationship with the Lord. How do we accomplish this?

Abiding in Him

In addition to seeking God for His power, for years I sought Him for His glory, or manifested presence in my life. My motive for my prayer was not right many times. However, I knew that abiding in Him was the key to moving in authority and power. Even though I did not have any results, I knew glory was something I could obtain. God had me in John 15, for years learning about abiding in Him. I knew that this abiding in Him would cause me to be one with Him and I thought this was how I would experience the glory of God, authority and power. My favorite Scripture during this time was Psalms 27: 4:

> One thing have I desired of the Lord, that will I seek after;
> that I may dwell in the house of the Lord all the days of
> my life, to behold the beauty of the Lord, and to inquire
> in His temple.

We see in this Scripture that David sought to dwell in His house all the days of His life. I believed the result of this would cause him to behold God and to inquire or receive revelation in His temple. This scripture gave me hope because I knew God was not a respecter of persons.

Through my study of the Word I knew that in the Old Testament that the place where glory dwelled was in the tabernacle, in the Holy of Holies. In the New Testament, He is the Holy of Holies and in order for Christians to find glory or His presence they need to abide in Him. All of this became the foundation in my search for the glory of God. In the beginning I was seeking after an experience and what I found was Him. The Scripture is true; He is the beginning (Alpha) and end (Omega). I sought glory and found Him. When I sought His power I found He is power. He is the end of all our seeking. I also found that every true doctrine has to have the cross as its foundation. He is the beginning. If the doctrine of glory is true then I knew the way into it had to start with Jesus.

The Lord showed me that being one with Him came before we could behold His glory. So of myself I tried to abide which I thought was praying continually. It was after much prayer, fasting, frustration, guilt, and there was even a time I gave up on receiving the glory, that I realized that I could not bring myself into an abiding relationship with God. My cry was: "God I can't do this". I even heard preachers say we can't dwell continually with God. After several years of this the Lord gave me a great revelation that changed my life. The Lord showed me I Corinthians 1:29-30.

I Corinthians 1: 29-30 says:

> 29.
>
> *That no flesh should glory in His presence.*
>
> 30.
>
> But of Him are ye in Christ Jesus, *who of God is made unto us wisdom, and righteousness, and sanctification, and redemption.*

I found that by the Father we are in Christ Jesus. This changed my life forever. It is by the Father that I have an abiding relationship with Jesus. Remember to be in Him is to have His glory and to be made perfect in one. In John 15, the Father is called the husbandman or farmer. It is the husbandman that puts the branches on the vine who is Jesus. Romans 11:16-23, talks about how we were grafted in the tree. But how does God do this? The answer is in I Corinthians 1:30; Jesus is made unto us wisdom, righteousness, sanctification and redemption. When we realize we have these spiritual blessings because of the cross, we will experience, walk and behold the glory of God. These blessings lead us to holiness. Holiness leads us to the presence of God. When I walk in holiness, I receive His nature and God is able to manifest Himself to me because I am holy.

Hebrews 12: 14 says:

> *Follow peace with all men, and holiness, without which no*
> *man shall see the Lord.*

In the Old Testament, the Holy of Holies was the place in the tabernacle where God met the High Priest. It was the place where the glory came. In the New Testament times the Holy of Holies is when one comes into the presence of God.

Psalms 15: 1-2 says:

1.

> *Lord who shall abide in thy tabernacle? Who shall dwell in*
> *thy holy hill?*

2.

> *He that walketh uprightly, and worketh righteousness, and*
> *speaks the truth in His heart.*

Jesus being made wisdom, righteousness, sanctification, and redemption leads us to holiness which leads us to God.

When we talk about holiness today it has a bad connotation in some people's minds. Walking in holiness is not a bunch of does and don'ts but it is a glorious freedom God gives us. It allows us to be like Him.

What is holiness? It is the image of God. It is the difference between light and darkness, God being the light. It is as the difference between clean and dirty water, God being the clean water.

When we look at Ephesians 1:4 and 2 Peter 3:35, we see that we have a right to holiness. Holiness is part of our destiny.

Ephesians 1: 3-4 says:

> 3.
>
> *Blessed be the God and Father of our Lord Jesus Christ, who hath blessed us with **all spiritual blessings** in heavenly places in Christ:*
>
> 4.
>
> *According as **He hath chosen us in Him** before the foundation of the world **that we should be holy** and without blame **before Him in love**.*

We see here that we were chosen to be in Him before the foundation of the world. We are also, to be holy and before Him in love. What a glorious destiny.

2 Peter 1: 3-4 says:

>   3.

>   *According as His divine power hath given unto us **all things***
>   ***that pertain unto life and godliness**, through the knowledge*
>   *of Him that hath **called us to glory** and virtue.*

>   4.

>   *Whereby are given unto us exceeding great and precious*
>   *promises: that by these ye might be partakers of the **divine***
>   ***nature**, having escaped the corruption that is in the world*
>   *through lust.*

Peter says we have been given all things to be partakers of the divine nature. Paul in Ephesians says we have been given all spiritual blessings to be holy. If we put these scriptures together we see that we have been given all things to have the divine nature which is holiness. We see in Hebrews 12:14 and Ephesians 1:4, that with holiness we can see or know God, be in Him, in love, and be blameless.

We have been called before the foundation of the world to be holy and be in Him. We have been called to be like God. He made us in His image. Before the foundation of the world God said, "Let us make man in our own image". He did this by placing us in Christ, that we be holy and before Him in love. Holiness is the image of God. When the angels see God they cry "Holy", (Isaiah 6:3).

Holiness is like a spiritual magnet in that once we embrace holiness it will draw us to God. The enemy has tried to lie to us to make us think holiness is drudgery. As a church if we embrace holiness and call it a good thing we will come into contact with the glory of God as never before.

The question then becomes, how do we come into holiness? The answer is in I Corinthians 1:30; Jesus is made unto us wisdom, righteousness, sanctification, and redemption. These are what I call the keys to intimacy with God because they all lead us to holiness.

Let's look at these keys. First of all, wisdom that comes from Jesus leads us to holiness.

Proverbs 3:35 says:

> The **wise** inherit **glory**.

If wisdom leads to glory, then wisdom will lead us through holiness. The way to glory is through holiness. Remember we are chosen to be in Him (which is glory), to be holy and without blame. Being in Him makes me holy. Wisdom leads me to be in Him. If I were a mathematician and made an equation I could say,

> **Wisdom = Holiness**

The next key is righteousness. Paul exhorts us to be righteous in Romans 6:19.

Romans 6:19 says:

> Yield your members servants to righteousness unto holiness.

The fruit of righteousness is holiness, Romans 6:22. Therefore we can conclude that;

> **Righteousness = Holiness**

Hebrews 10:10 and, Colossians 1:22 together show us about the third key which is sanctification.

Hebrews 10:10 says:

> *By the which will we are **sanctified** through the offering of the **body of Jesus** Christ once for all.*

Colossians 1:22 says:

> *In the **body of His flesh** through death, to present you **holy and unblamable** and unreprovable in His sight.*

We see through these Scriptures that through the offering of His body we are sanctified which causes us to be holy. Therefore we can say:

> **Sanctification = Holiness**

We can learn about our fourth key which is redemption by looking at I Peter 1: 16-19,

> *16.*
>
> *… Be ye **holy**; for I am **holy**.*
>
> *18.*
>
> *…ye were not **redeemed** with corruptible things,*
>
> *19.*
>
> *But with the precious blood of Christ,*

We see God saying for us to be holy as He is holy. The Scripture goes on to say that we were redeemed by the precious blood of Jesus. So to be holy we must receive that we are redeemed. We are part of His family because of the blood of Jesus, Revelation 5:9. We can therefore make the conclusion that:

Redemption = Holiness

If we break I Corinthians 1:30, down into a mathematical equation it would be:

Wisdom + Righteousness + Sanctification + Redemption = Holiness

We are righteous because of the sacrifice of His body and flesh on the cross (2 Corinthians 5:21). We are sanctified by the offering of His body. We are redeemed by the shedding of His blood.

John 6:56 says:

*He that eateth my flesh, and drinketh my blood **dwelleth in me**, and I in Him.*

When I receive or eat and drink all that is mine because of the cross: (wisdom, righteousness, sanctification and redemption), then I am holy. Because I am holy I will dwell in Him which is the glory of God, and He will dwell in me by His Holy Spirit.

Let's look at righteousness closer.

Psalms 140:13 says:

> *The **upright** shall dwell in thy presence.*

Song of Solomon 1:4 says:

> *The **upright** love thee.*

If we look at the entire book of Romans 8, it starts off showing us that there is no condemnation to them which are in Christ. The reason for this is because we are righteous because of the sacrifice of Jesus. Because of this sacrifice there is no place for guilt, because we are forgiven. The chapter ends asking the question: "What shall separate us from the love of God?" The conclusion is nothing can separate us from His love. Why is this so? It is because we are righteous. Righteousness means that there is no separation between us and God.

2 Corinthians 5:21 says:

> *For He hath made Him to be **sin**; that we might be made the **righteousness of God in Him**.*

Righteousness means I do not have to sin. The enemy can not make me sin. But when I receive that I am righteous it is then my choice as to whether or not I sin. I am free from sin, and the fruit of this is holiness, which is having His nature. If I have His nature then it will be natural for me to be where He is, which is in His presence.

The rights of the righteous are:

- Healing – I Peter 2:24:

  > *Who His own self bare our sins in His own body on the tree, that we Being dead to sins, should live unto **righteousness**: By whose stripes ye **were healed**.*

Because I am now righteous, I was healed at the cross. My other rights of being righteous are:

- Prosperity – Psalms 35:27:

*Let them shout for joy, and be glad, that favor my **righteous** cause: yea, be magnified, which hath pleasure I the **prosperity of His servant**.*

Psalms 112: 2-3 says:

2.

*His seed shall be mighty upon the earth: the generation of the **upright** will be **blessed**.*

3.

***Wealth and riches** shall be in his **house**:and his **righteousness** endureth forever.*

Others Scriptures are: II Corinthians 8:9, Psalms 37:34, Psalms 84:11.

- Reign in life and no condemnation – Romans 5:17-19, and Romans 8:1.
- The presence and love of God – Psalms 15, Psalms 17:15, Psalms 23, Song of Solomon 1:4; Psalms 140:13 says, "***The upright shall dwell in thy presence**.*"

Sanctification is our next key to entering into the glory of God. Sanctification through the sacrifice of the body of Jesus has a couple of functions. When we are sanctified we are made clean.

John 17:17 says:

Sanctify them through thy truth: Thy **word** is truth.

John 15:3 says:

*Now ye are **clean** through the **word** which I have spoken unto you.*

When we receive the word of God which states in Hebrews 10:10, that the flesh of Jesus sanctifies us, we are made clean. Another function of sanctification is that it removes the consciousness of sin, (Hebrews 9:13-14). This means we are not conscious of, or thinking about sin or our shortcomings. What we become conscious of is the presence of God. We start to walk in the spirit and not the flesh. In 2 Chronicles 7:15-16, we see that our prayers are heard because we are sanctified. In verse 15, it says God's eyes and ears are open to the prayer that comes from the temple. In our case we are the temple. In verse 16, we see the reason our prayers are heard is because God has chosen and sanctified this house. We see that sanctification also brings us to the place where we can use His name. This is the place of authority. Another blessing of sanctification happens when we combine it with our being righteous. When these two come together confidence is birthed. This is the place of answered prayer.

I John 3:21-22 says:

21.

Beloved if our heart condemn us not, then we have confidence toward God.

22.

And whatsoever we ask, we receive of Him, because we keep His commandments, and do those things that are pleasing in His sight.

Our heart does not condemn us when we walk in our sanctification. In this place we also know we are pleasing to God, not because of what we do, but because of receiving the sacrifice of Jesus. However, there is a perfection process we must all go through where He will perfect our hearts. During this perfecting God does not want us to be in guilt or beat ourselves up. What we need to do is to ask for forgiveness and run back to the Father. I remember reading a book by Brother Lawrence, Practicing the Presence of God. Brother Lawrence said he did not dwell on his failures. When he fell he went humbly to God and asked for forgiveness. He would say, "Father if you leave me to myself I will fall." We must look to the Father to keep us from falling and bring us faultless into the presence of His glory (Jude 24).

Righteousness and sanctification allow me to be confident in God. Earlier I showed how we are redeemed by the blood of Jesus, which allows us to be holy or have God's nature.

If we look deeper we see that through redemption I receive the adoption of being a son of God. I have been grafted into the vine, who is Jesus. I am in Him; I am part of the family of God. When I receive the blood of Jesus, I become part of the bloodline of God the Father.

Galatians 4:5 says:

> To **redeem** them that were under the law, that we might receive the adoption of sons.

Galatians 4:7 says:

> *Wherefore thou art no more a servant, but a son: if a son, then*
> *an heir of God through Christ.*

To be an heir of God means that whatever God has is mine. I am a joint-heir with Jesus and whatever He has is mine also.

How do we come into the glory of God, the presence of God? It is by God that we are in Him, because Jesus is made unto us wisdom, righteousness, sanctification, and redemption (I Corinthians 1:30). Remember the mathematical equation:

Wisdom + Righteousness + Sanctification + Redemption = Holiness

I tried to abide and come into the presence of God of myself but I could not do it. When I realized it was by God that I was in Him this changed my life and I found myself in His presence. Paul, I believe had the same testimony.

Philippians 3: 8-9 says:

8.

> *Yea doubtless, and I count all things but loss for excellency of the*
> *knowledge of Christ Jesus my Lord: for whom I have suffered*
> *the loss of all things, and do count them but dung, that I may*
> *win Christ,*

9.

> ***And be found in Him***, *not having mine own* ***righteousness**,*
> *which is of the law, but that which is through* ***the faith of***
> ***Christ, the righteousness*** *which is of* ***God by faith**.*

Paul, found himself in Christ once he realized he was righteous through the righteousness which is of God by faith in Christ. Once you go through this process you too will find yourself in Him. In John 6:56, Jesus said, "*He that eats my flesh and drinks my blood, dwells in me, and I in him.*" When we eat or receive what His blood and flesh does for us at the cross, this enables us to dwell in Him (glory), and He is in us. This has nothing to do with what we do; this is so no flesh will glory in His presence, I Corinthians 1:29. However, we like Paul must seek Him with our all. As we seek Him with our all eventually we will find Him. It is during the seeking process where He teaches us about His wisdom, righteousness, sanctification and redemption. This is the normal life. We can abide in Him, it is not impossible. We can dwell in His house all the days of our lives, and it is possible to behold His glory on a continual basis. This is a supernatural wonder that God wants to work in all of us. Hebrew 10: 19-23, sums up how we come into the presence or glory of God. Keep in mind that glory is the manifestation of God in our lives, and we are the temple of the living God.

Hebrews 10: 19-23 says:

19.

*Having therefore, brethren, boldness to enter into the holiest (**holiness**) by the blood of Jesus(**Redemption**),*

20.

*By a new and living way, which He consecrated for us, through the veil that is to say, His flesh (**Sanctification**);*

21.

And having a high priest over the house of God;

22.

Let us draw near with a true heart in full assurance of faith, (**confidence/righteousness**) *having our hearts sprinkled from an evil conscience, and our bodies washed with pure water* (**sanctification**).

23.

Let us hold fast the profession of our faith without wavering: (for He is faithful that promised;)

This passage shows we come into holiness, through righteousness, sanctification and redemption. As Paul said, "Where is the boasting?" God has already done it. When wisdom, righteousness, sanctification, and redemption come together in us, they produce faith. This is the power of the gospel.

Romans 1: 16-17 says:

16.

For I am not ashamed of the gospel of Christ: for it is the power of God unto salvation to everyone that believeth;

17.

For therein is the righteousness of God revealed from faith to faith: as it is written, **the just live by faith.**

Hebrews 10:38 says, that the just live by faith and if any man draw back, my soul shall have no pleasure in him. When faith is produced I am able to stay in His presence. If I leave His presence then God is not pleased, because to depart His presence is unbelief (Hebrews 3:12).

As I receive His wisdom, righteousness, sanctification, and redemption then the way for me to abide is open to me. If I am in Him then I am in heavenly places in Christ Jesus and authority and power belong to me because all principalities and powers are under my feet because they are under Jesus' feet.

The way of authority

Because of the cross I can abide in Him. When I abide in Him I come under His authority. James 4:8 says to draw near to God and God will draw near to us. He then says resist the devil and he will flee from us. The enemy flees when we are near God. This is because we come under God's authority which places the enemy under our authority. The centurion, whose servant was healed by Jesus, said he knew Jesus could heal by speaking the word. This was because the centurion was under authority; therefore, he had authority to tell one to come and another to go. Jesus called this great faith. It is the same for us: We only have authority when we are under His authority. We are to be directed by Him in whatever we do. When we abide in Him in the heavenly places the enemy is under our authority. The way to authority is open to us because of the blood of Jesus, and we are seated in Him in heavenly places.

The way to power

What about the power of God? Paul says in Philippians 3: 8-10, He suffered the loss of all things to win Christ. He goes on to say that He found himself in Him by the righteousness which comes from God. He found himself in the abiding relationship with God. In verse 10, we see the results of being found in Him. They are the following;

1. To know Him.
2. To know the *power* of resurrection.
3. To be made conformable to His death.

He shows that the way to know the power of His resurrection is to be in Him. We also see that a result of being in His glory is the power of God (Ephesians 3:16-20). To come into His glory or His presence is to realize the manifest presence of God in your life.

Isaiah 40:10 says that when the Lord comes, He comes in power. Jesus is called the power of God in I Corinthians 1: 24. When the Father and Jesus come and make their abode with us we come into a place of power. So we see that we come into authority and power because of the cross of Jesus Christ. We can not do anything to receive it in the flesh, but we must just receive the finished work of Christ on the cross.

The church has a right to move in authority and power because of the sacrifice of Jesus. We have no excuse. Didn't Daniel say that he saw the saints inherit the kingdom and dominion? I believe dominion is moving in authority and power. It is time for the church to receive her inheritance of authority and power. We can do the greater works. Abiding in Him is our foundation for us moving in the authority and power of God. Since Jesus is our model let's look at how He moved in authority and power, so this will become practical in our lives.

Chapter 3

JESUS OUR MODEL

Faith works by love. Galatians 5:6

The foundation of Jesus' ministry was that He walked in love. In John 15:10, Jesus says, "If ye keep my commandments, ye shall abide in my love; even as I have kept my Father's commandments, and abide in His love." Jesus looked at the love of the Father as a place to dwell. Jesus also said that it was His meat to do the will of God. His motive was to always bring God glory. Not only did Jesus walk in love, but he was anointed with power.

> *How God **anointed** Jesus of Nazareth with the **Holy Ghost** and with **power**: who went about doing good, and **healing all** that were oppressed of the devil, **for God was with Him**. Acts 10:38*

This Scripture is key in seeing how Jesus, our model, moved in authority and power on the earth. There are three components to this scripture;

1. Jesus was anointed with the Holy Ghost.

2. Jesus was anointed with power.

3. God was with Him.

In Luke 3:22, we see that Jesus received the Holy Spirit.

Luke 3:22 says:

> *And the Holy Ghost descended in bodily shape like a dove upon Him, and a voice came from heaven, which said, Thou art my beloved Son, in thee I am well pleased.*

So when Jesus receives the Holy Spirit that is God in Him. Jesus then goes into the wilderness full of the Holy Spirit, and is tempted by Satan. In Luke 4:14, it says, "And Jesus returned in the power of the Spirit. This is when He was anointed with power. To be anointed means that there is an impartation or an empowerment from God to complete certain tasks. The difference from a speaker in the natural or flesh versus an anointed speaker is that the anointed speaker gets his inspiration from God, when they are yielded to Him. The anointing of power working with the Holy Spirit in us allows us to move successfully in ministry.

The anointing is God's promise to be with you though the Holy Spirit, in whatever capacity that the anointing is given. However, you can be anointed with the Holy Spirit and power but be separated from God the Father. We will see this more in depth in chapter 4.

If we look at Luke 4:18, we see the power Jesus was anointed with.

Luke 4:18-19 says:

18.

> *The Spirit of the Lord is upon me, because He hath anointed*
> *me to **preach the gospel** to the poor; He hath sent me **to heal***
> *the broken-hearted, **to preach deliverance** to the captives,*
> *and **recovering of sight to the blind, to set at liberty** those*
> *that are bruised.*

19.

> *To **preach** the acceptable year of the Lord.*

Jesus was anointed to preach, heal, bring deliverance, and work miracles. These were some of His power anointings. However, these were not enough for Jesus to move in power and authority as God wanted.

Acts 10:38, says; "Jesus was anointed with the Holy Spirit and with power. He went about doing good, healing all that were oppressed of the devil." Why is this so? It is because of the last part of this verse. Jesus was able to do all this because God was with Him. God being with Him was the key to Jesus being successful in ministry. What does it mean to have God with you?

Jesus says in John 15:10:

> *If ye keep my commandments ye shall abide in in my love; even*
> *as I have kept my Father's commands and abide in His love.*

Jesus had an abiding relationship with the Father. According to John 14:10, Jesus said He was in the Father, and the Father was in Him.

Jesus was in perfect oneness with God. When you are in this place of oneness you keep His commands and the Father comes and makes His abode with us. This is the place of coming into the glory of God. We know Jesus experienced this because the Scripture says God was with Him. It was not enough for Jesus to be anointed with the Holy Ghost and power, but Jesus knew God the Father was with Him. He walked in the glory of God.

Jesus moved in the fullness of God. When you are baptized with the Holy Spirit, and you receive some giftings or power to do certain things you minister in part if you're not walking in love. This is the message of I Corinthians 13. The anointing or gifting is not what it should be without love. However, when He comes and we abide in Him who is perfect and we put away the childish things, which are the giftings in this passage. Then we will not move in part anymore, because we will come into the fullness of God. The fullness of God is knowing God Himself is with you.

We see this in I Corinthians 13:9-12:

9.

For we know in part, and we prophesy in part.

10.

But when that which is perfect is come, then that which is in part shall be done away.

11.

*When I was a child, I spake as a child: but when I became a man I put away childish things. (**The gifts of God**)*

12.

> For now we see through a glass, darkly: but then face to face:
> now I know in part; but then shall I know even as also I am
> known.

2 Corinthians 3: 18, says:

> But we all, with open face beholding as in a glass the glory
> of the Lord, are changed into the same image **from glory to
> glory**, even as by the Spirit of the Lord.

When we come into glory there is a power that comes with God. God showed me that with each level of glory there is corresponding power. This is the power Jesus walked in while on earth.

Jesus knew God was with Him. This was His faith focus. His focus was not on the ministry that needed to be done but His focus was on the fact that God was with Him. Isn't this what faith is? Hebrews 11: 6 says, "But without faith it is impossible to please Him: for He that cometh to God must believe that His is, and that He is a rewarder of them that diligently seek Him." The passage states that faith says, "He is." I like to say, faith says that He is present with me. When I know this I know I can pray and ask what I will and know He will answer because I know He has heard me. The Scripture says if we know He has heard us then we have what we asked for (I John 5:14-15).

Jesus had the Holy Spirit, was anointed with power and God was with Him. These were the keys to His power. However, there was another aspect Jesus had that made Him successful in ministry. This aspect was that He glorified God.

Glorifying God

Jesus motive for all He does to this present day is to bring God glory. To bring God glory or to glorify Him means to please or to bring pleasure to the Father. The Lord showed me that to glorify God means to cause a shout or rejoicing to go off in heaven. The Scripture says that the angels rejoice when one is saved (Luke 15:10). This shows rejoicing goes on in heaven when certain events take place on earth. This is also true when we glorify God through praise and worship. God says He inhabits our praise, our praise goes up and He wraps it around Him like a coat. I used to ask God what do we do when the Father and Jesus come to us? The answer is to glorify God. God does not want anyone to glory in His presence. We are to glorify Him. To this day the purpose of Jesus is to glorify the Father.

John 15:8 says:

> *Herein is my Father* **glorified***, that ye bear much fruit; so shall ye be my disciples.*

How is the Father glorified? We see Jesus say in John 15:7, that when we abide, we can ask what we will, He will answer, and the Father is glorified by this. We also see that Jesus was a true worshipper because His heart or His motive is to glorify God. The following scriptures will show why this is true;

John 4: 23-24 says:

> *23.*

> *But the hour cometh, and now is, when the true worshippers*

shall worship the Father in spirit and in truth; for the Father seeketh such to worship Him.

24.

God is a Spirit: and they that worship Him must worship Him in spirit and in truth.

This Scripture shows that God is looking for those who are true worshippers. We see that Jesus was a true worshipper because of the following scriptures, and these were key to Him moving in authority and power while on the earth.

John 5:30-31 says:

30.

*I can of mine **own self do nothing**: as I hear, I judge: and my judgment is just; **because I seek not mine own will**, but the will of the Father which hath sent me.*

31.

*If I bear witness of myself, my witness is not **true**.*

John 7:17-18 says:

17.

If any man will do His will, He shall know of the doctrine, whether it be of God, or whether I speak of myself.

18.

He that speaketh of himself seeketh his own glory: but he that seeketh His glory that sent him, the same is **true**, and **no unrighteousness** is in him.

Jesus is saying the following;

1. He did not seek His own will, but sought after God's will.

This means that Jesus came under the authority of the Father and therefore had authority. He did not exalt Himself, therefore God considered Him true. When you seek His will for a situation you are asking for His strategy for the circumstance you are dealing with.

2. He sought to bring God glory. This is His motive, and because of this He is considered as true. Remember God is looking for true worshippers. The way to this is to seek His will and to seek to bring Him glory. He is seeking after those with these qualities.

The Scripture shows us that God inhabits the praises of His people; this refers to praise and worship. These are ways we give God glory. But if our life is to be as Jesus where we seek His will and to bring Him glory, God will find us because we are true worshippers. When this becomes our life we will know God is with us. This was the foundation to the ministry of Jesus. As the Scripture says there is no unrighteousness in true worshippers. When we embrace that we are righteous by faith in Jesus we will start to walk in being a true worshipper. Some may say, "Well how does all of this relate to moving in authority and power?" Psalms 29 gives us some insight into this.

Psalms 29:1-5, &10-11:

1.

Give unto the Lord, O ye mighty *give unto the Lord glory and strength.*

2.

Give unto the Lord the glory due unto His name; worship the Lord in the beauty of holiness.

3.

The voice of the Lord is upon the waters: the God of glory thundereth; the Lord is upon many waters.

4.

The voice of the Lord is **powerful***; the voice of the Lord is full of majesty.*

5.

The voice of the Lord breaketh the cedars; Yea, the Lord breaketh the Cedars of Lebanon.

10.

The Lord sitteth upon the flood, yea, the the Lord sitteth King forever.

11.

The Lord will give strength (power) unto His people; the Lord will bless His people with peace.

This Scripture shows that we glorify the Lord in a place of holiness. The author says glorify the Lord in the beauty of holiness. As we saw before to enter into holiness we must receive what Jesus did for us at the cross. By Him we are in Him and Jesus is made unto us wisdom, righteousness, sanctification, and redemption (I Corinthians 1:30). When I receive this I walk in holiness, and I am in the presence or glory of God. It is here that we like Jesus must seek His will and seek to bring Him glory. He sought to bring Him glory. This should be our prayer. When we worship Him in the beauty of holiness, we come to the point when the voice of the Lord is released. Think of what the centurion said, "Speak the word only and my servant will be healed." When we are looking for His will, looking to bring Him glory in a situation, and God is with us, He will release the word for a situation. This is when authority and power is released.

Psalms 29:11 says, "That God will give strength or power to His people. This happens by releasing the word that God has spoken. Paul asks the question in Galatians 3:5, how are miracles done.

Galatians 3:5 says:

5.

*He therefore that **ministereth to you the Spirit, and worketh miracles** among you, doeth He it by the works of the law, or by **the hearing of faith.***

Jesus moved by the hearing of faith. In John 5:30, He says, "I can of my own self do nothing: as I hear, I judge: and my judgment is just;

because I seek not mine own will, but the will of the Father which hath
sent me."

John 14:10 says:

> Believest thou not that I am in the Father, and the Father
> in me? The words that I speak *unto you I speak not of myself:*
> **but the Father that dwelleth in me He doeth the works.**

Jesus waited for God's will in a situation and then God moved on
Jesus behalf. God moved because Jesus is a true worshipper, and He
glorified the Father.

Jesus tells the disciples in John 14:13, that whatever they ask for
in His name He will do it, so that the Father may be glorified in the
Son.

John 15:7-8 says:

7.

> *If ye abide in me, and my words abide in you, ye shall ask what*
> *ye will, and it shall be done unto you.*

8.

> *Herein is my Father glorified, that ye bear much fruit; so shall*
> *ye be my disciples.*

Even today Jesus' reason for answering our prayers is so the Father
will be glorified in the Son. Jesus says we are His disciples when we abide
in Him. We are his disciples when we seek to do His will and glorify
God. When we do this God will be with us as He was with Jesus.

The keys to Jesus moving in authority and power were:

1. He was anointed with the Holy Spirit.

2. He was anointed with power.

3. God was with Him.

We are to move in ministry the same way Jesus did. Remember that the foundation to Jesus ministry is love.

Ephesians 3: 16-20, says:

16.

That he would grant you, according to the riches of his glory, to be strengthened with might by his Spirit in the inner man;

17.

That Christ may dwell in your hearts by faith; that ye, being rooted and grounded in love,

18.

May be able to comprehend with all saints what is the breadth, and length, and depth, and height;

19.

*And to know **the love of Christ**, which passeth knowledge, that ye might be filled with all the fullness of God.*

20.

*Now unto him that is able to do exceeding abundantly above all that we ask or think, according to the **power that worketh in us**,*

When we experience the riches of glory, or the riches in being in His presence, we will realize that Christ is in us. This is beyond having the baptism of the Holy Spirit. There is a door opened in the spirit where you know Christ is in you. This is how we behold His glory. He is in us. It is like hearing in the Spirit. Even though, God could speak to us in an audible voice so we could hear it in the natural, most times the voice is in us. So it is with beholding the Lord. We can experience an outward vision of the Lord, but most times we experience Him in us.

When I realize Christ is in me, I am rooted and grounded in the love of God. The Lord will cause you to realize that you are in His heart. Then you are abiding in love. The Scripture says that when I know love I will be filled with the fullness of God. I realize that not only is Christ in me, but I can experience the Father in me also. When I have his fullness I have His eyes, ears and heart. In 2 Chronicles 7:14-18, the people are told that when they seek God's face He would give His eyes, ears and heart. They would also have the answer to prayer. This is the kingdom of God, because we have come to the Father and Jesus (Hebrews 12: 22- 28).

By walking in love I realize that the Father and Christ is in me, because of this the power of God is in me. This is why the Lord is able to do exceeding abundantly above all we ask or think according to the power that works in us (Ephesians 3:20). Christ in us is the power of God. What the Lord showed years ago was true, the power was in me. I sought for power and found Jesus.

This is why we can do the greater works, because Jesus went to the Father. We are to move as Jesus did. Jesus said, "The words I speak unto you I speak not of myself: but the Father that dwells in me, He does the works" (John 14:10). This is why we are told in James 5:15 that the prayer of faith shall save the sick, and the Lord shall raise him up. As I walk in love I will realize that the power of God is in me. This is why love is the foundation to moving in the authority and power of God.

Chapter 4

WHY COULDN'T WE HEAL?
THE EXAMPLE OF THE DISCIPLES

We are the disciples of Jesus when we abide in Him as He abided in the Father. We are His disciples when we seek to do His will, and when we seek to glorify the Father. As He is so are we in this world. How is He in this world? His purpose right now is to glorify the Father. If we are to be like Him that must be our motive and our call also. This is all part of loving Him and being a true worshipper.

The apostles were the disciples of Jesus yet they found themselves in a situation where there was no answer to their prayer, of healing a young boy. When Jesus came out of the Mount of Transfiguration He went and healed the boy. Afterwards the disciples came to Him and said, "Why couldn't we heal the boy? They asked the question because they knew they had authority and power yet they could not heal in this instance. Let's look at this story because it is an example to us in how to walk in authority and power.

An example from the disciples

I believe Luke 9, gives us an example of how we come into the glory of God. The glory of God is the light that surrounds God. It is coming into His presence. Glory is the clothes that God wears. Glory is the tunnel that leads us to the kingdom and power of God. Walking in glory is coming into the abiding place with God. The Lord showed me that each level of glory has a corresponding level of power. So in order for us to walk in the fullness of His power we must learn how to come into His glory.

Luke 9:1-2, 6 says:

1.

Then He called His twelve disciples together, and gave them power and authority over all devils, and cure diseases.

2.

And He sent them to preach the Kingdom of God, and to heal the sick.

6.

And they departed and went through the towns, preaching the gospel and healing everywhere.

Here were men that were anointed by Jesus to heal the sick and preach the kingdom of God. They preached and healed everywhere. When they come back they told Jesus about what they did. This was probably a thrilling experience for them to preach and heal the sick.

These were men that people did not look up to; they were fishermen and tax collectors. However, now they moved in power and authority. This probably gave them a great boost of confidence. However, Jesus does not let them relax in their new status. He did not let them get satisfied in their new place in God. In Luke 9:18, He asks them who do people say I am. Peter answered that Jesus was the Christ, the Son of the living God. In Matthew 16:17, Jesus says, "Flesh and blood has not revealed this to you, but my Father which is in heaven." The significance of these passages is that here were men who preached and healed the sick, yet they did not know Jesus, only Peter was able to answer the question. In Luke 9:23-27, Jesus proceeds to show the disciples the way to knowing Him. Romans 10:17, shows us that faith comes by hearing and hearing the word of God. If this is the case then Jesus had to show them the way to hearing God, to come to a place of faith.

Luke 9: 23-27 says:

23.

> And He said to them all, If any man will come after me, let him deny himself, and take up His cross daily, and follow me.

24.

> For whosoever will save his life shall lose it: but whosoever will loss His life for my sake, the same shall save it.

25.

> For what is a man advantaged, if He gain the whole world, and lose himself, and be cast away?

26.

For whosoever shall be ashamed of me and my words of him
shall the Son of man be ashamed, **when He shall come in His**
own glory, and in His Father's and of the holy angels.

27.

But I tell you of a truth, there be some standing here, which
shall not taste of death till **they see the kingdom of God**.

Mark 9:1 says:

And He said unto them, Verily I say unto you, That there be
some of them that stand here, which shall not taste of death, till
they have seen the **kingdom of God come with power.**

When I used to read Luke 9:23, this Scripture would bother me, because I did not want to deny myself. The denying of self will open many doors for the church. In verse 23, Jesus is telling the disciples to deny themselves daily and to follow or seek after Him with everything they have. In verse 25, He shows them that even if they gained the world it would not be worth losing Him. He then goes on and says," If your ashamed of me and my words, in this adulterous and sinful generation, of him also shall the Son of man be ashamed, when He comes in His own glory, and in His Father's, and of the holy angels," Mark 8:38, and Luke 9:26. Jesus uses the words ashamed and adulterous together, because the spirit of adultery causes one to be ashamed of the one you are with whether a husband, wife, or God. I John 2:15, says that if we love the world the love of God is not in us. It is that simple.

James 4:4, says:

> *Ye adulterers and adulteresses, know ye not that the friendship of the world is enmity with God? Whosoever therefore will be a friend of the world is the enemy of God.*

Jesus said, "If you are ashamed of me I will be ashamed of you when I come in my glory, the Fathers glory and of the angel's glory." Jesus was prophesying to the disciples. He said if you deny yourself, and seek me then He will not be ashamed of them when He comes in glory. In other words, if they deny themselves and seek Him they would experience the glory of God. Jesus was not just talking about when they go to heaven but He was talking about in their lifetime.

We know this because of Luke 9:27, it says:

> *But I tell you of a truth, there be some standing here, which shall not taste of death, till they see the kingdom of God.*

He was telling them that if they deny themselves and seek Him daily they could experience His kingdom, glory, and power now. Daniel said he saw the saints come into the kingdom and dominion of God. Jesus was saying this experience was for now and He is saying the same thing to us today.

If we look at Hebrews 12:22-24, & 28, we see the kingdom of God described.

Hebrews 12:22-24 & 28:

22.

> *But ye are come unto Mount Zion, and unto the city of the*

*living God, the heavenly Jerusalem, and to an **innumerable*** *
company of angels,*

23.

To the general assembly and church of the firstborn, which are *
written in heaven, **and to God** the Judge of all, and to the* *
spirit, of just men made perfect.*

24.

And to Jesus *the mediator of the new covenant, and to the* *
blood of sprinkling, that speaketh better things than that of* *
Abel.*

28.

Wherefore we receiving a kingdom which cannot *
moved.*

Coming into the kingdom is coming to a place in God where the Father and Jesus are manifested to you, and you are living in a state where this is your daily experience. This is possible for you. John 14:21 says, "He that hath my commandments, and keepth them, he it is that loveth me (not ashamed of Him), and he that loveth and shall be loved of my Father, and I will love Him, and will manifest myself to him.

John 14:23 says, "We will come unto him and make our abode with him." We enter into the kingdom when they come to us. How do they come to us? Jesus said, "When I come in my glory, my Father's glory and the angel's glory." Glory is as a tunnel, bridge that leads us to God. As

I walk in glory, I become a partaker of the kingdom of God. The glory and the kingdom are not separate. When I come into glory I become part of the kingdom. Revelations 21: 10-11, and Hebrews 12:22, both talk about the heavenly or the holy Jerusalem. Revelations 3, calls the holy Jerusalem the bride of Christ. This is the kingdom of God, and we see in Revelations 21:11, that this kingdom has the glory of God as her light. When He comes to us then we are partakers of His glory and kingdom. Some do not partake in this experience because the kingdom of God is taken by force. We are told to seek first the kingdom and all else will be added to us. What is the kingdom? It is the Father and Jesus coming to us, and we, His people, staying or abiding in Him by faith.

Glory is like the clothes that God wears. Psalms 91:1 says that," he that dwells in the secret place of the most High shall abide under the shadow of the Almighty." Our shadows are dark but He has a shadow of light and life. The glory, kingdom and power are not separate entities, but when we touch glory we touch them all. They are only separate for sake of definition. Matthew 6:13 says, "Thine is the kingdom, power and glory." In other words, He is the kingdom, power and glory. Jesus told the disciples they would see the kingdom and glory, and they saw Jesus and the Father in glory.

I Corinthians 1:24, says that Christ is the power of God. When Moses asked God to show him glory, God showed Moses Himself. God is the Father of glory, Ephesians 1:17. Jesus said the kingdom is likened to a land owner who leaves his land to people to watch. The land owner comes back and rewards the laborers according to their work. He is the landowner who comes back to us. The Father and Jesus are the focus of the kingdom, because all authority and power belong to them.

Jesus wanted the disciples to go beyond the power and authority they received, and come into the glory and the kingdom of God. He wanted them to come into the fullness of God. The Scripture says eight days later after He said deny yourselves, Jesus took Peter, John and James up into a mountain to pray. In Luke 9:31, they saw Moses, and Elijah appear with Jesus in glory. Luke 9:32, says they saw His glory. Did not Jesus say if they denied themselves and were not ashamed of Him they would experience glory?

In Luke 9:34-35, it says, "While He thus spoke, there came a cloud, and overshadowed them: and they feared as they entered into the cloud. And there came a voice out of the cloud saying, this is my beloved Son hear Him. At this point Peter, John and James saw the glory of God and God declared Jesus was His Son. In 2 Peter 1:16, Peter describes this experience as being eyewitnesses of His majesty or royalty. It was at this point they saw the Father and Son together and what they saw was the kingdom of God. The Father told them to hear Him and to be obedient. During this instance, Peter, John and James experience the glory, the kingdom and the dominion. They realize Jesus is the fullness of God. He is the kingdom, power and glory of God. He is the end of our seeking.

The previous passage shows that the denial of self is not to be drudgery but a blessing. Faith says He is and is a rewarder of them that diligently seek Him. The reward of denial is glory and the kingdom of God. Isn't that a blessing?

When they come out of the mountain they came to the other disciples who cannot heal a boy with an unclean spirit. Jesus heals the boy and the disciples want to know why they could not. Jesus calls them faithless and perverse.

How could they be faithless? Here were men of power and authority that healed all. Yet Jesus said they were faithless. They were faithless because the focus of faith is not to be on the thing you are asking for in prayer. The focus of our faith must be on Jesus. Hebrews 11:1 says:

> *Now faith is the substance of things hoped for, the evidence of things not seen.*

I Timothy 1:1, says, "Jesus is our hope." So if Jesus is the focus of this scripture then the substance of things hoped for is Jesus. The evidence of things not seen is the cross. We may not have been eyewitnesses to the cross, but we know through the Spirit and His word that Jesus was raised from the dead. Hebrews 11:1 goes with Hebrew 11:6, that says:

> *Without faith it is impossible to please God, for you must believe He is and is a rewarder of them that diligently seek Him.*

If I am diligently seeking Him then He is the substance of things I am hoping for, and I have it because of the evidence of things not seen (the cross). I used to look at this scripture and think that He would give me what I wanted if I sought after it hard enough. But the focus of these scriptures is Jesus. When I believe He is, then I have faith.

The disciples were faithless because there was a disconnect between them and God. Hebrews 3:12 says:

Take heed, brethren, lest there be in any of you an evil heart of unbelief, in departing from the living God.

Faith comes by hearing and hearing by the word of God. Remember Jesus told them to deny themselves and follow or seek Him to come into the glory and kingdom of God. These disciples were not there on the Mount of Transfiguration to hear God say this is my Son. They were perverse because they were satisfied with the power and authority they had and did not seek Jesus on a deeper level. They were perverse because they loved the world more. Look at Judas, his focus was on something else. The disciples may have loved the praise of men more, but there was something in their heart that caused a separation between them and God, or Jesus would not have said they were perverse.

In I Corinthians 13, Paul says that if we move in our gifting or anointing and do not have love, it is as nothing. If we do not have love we minister in part. In other words, the ministry is not what it should be. This was the disciple's case.

The disciples said why could we not heal and Jesus said because of unbelief. What is unbelief? Hebrews 3:12, says, "Take heed, brethren, lest there be in any of you an evil heart of unbelief, in departing form the living God." Leaving His presence is moving in unbelief. Matthew 17:20 says:

And Jesus said unto them, Because of your unbelief: for verily I say unto you, If ye have faith as a grain of mustard seed, ye shall say unto this mountain, Remove here to yonder place; and it shall remove, and nothing shall be impossible unto you.

If we know just a little bit that He is with us this is faith, and we can move mountains. Remember faith says He is with me.

Matthew 17:21 says, "Howbeit this kind goeth not out but by prayer and fasting." He did not tell them to fast and pray to cast out that type of demon. Fasting and prayer was to bring them to a higher level of faith.

Isaiah 58: 6 & 8 says:

6.

> *Is not this the **fast** that I have chosen? To loose the bands of wickedness, to undo the heavy burdens, and to let the oppressed go free, and ye break every yoke?*

8.

> *Then shall thy light break forth as the morning, and thine health shall spring forth speedily: and **thy righteousness** shall go before thee; the **glory of the Lord shall be thy rearward**.*

Fasting and prayer brings us to righteousness and the glory of God which is His presence. Our faith makes us righteous. We will then see the mountains in our lives move, because we know He is with us. Psalms 97:5 says the mountains melt at the presence of God.

Denying yourself, prayer, fasting and seeking Him will lead us to the glory, the kingdom and the power of God. Isn't this what Daniel saw? It is for the saints to inherit the kingdom, power and glory of God.

The Lord showed me that He wants to heal the blind, the deaf, and all manner of sickness and disease. However, He is limited because of the level of glory we are at. The greater the levels of glory you experience, the closer to God you are. Each level of glory has a corresponding level of power. The disciples had power yet there was a higher place for them to reach for, which comes by fasting and prayer.

As children of the Most High we need to start to ask God why we can't heal or deliver. Ask Him why our prayers are not answered. When we do this He will answer and help us get to the point where whatever we ask will be answered so God can be glorified through the Son.

PART II –
Moving in Authority and Power

Chapter 5

HAVE YOU EVER SEEN A TREE HEAL ANYBODY?

To move in authority and power the Father gives us several points of confidence that we can stand on, so that when we pray we will know God will move. Our first point of confidence comes from John 15:7, which says:

> If ye abide in me, and my words abide in you, ye Shall ask what ye will, and it shall be done unto you.

Abiding in Him is the place we need to be so that we know our prayers will be answered. We have seen how Jesus and His disciples moved in authority and power. We believe the disciples moved in this realm because they are in the bible, or they were a special class of people. However, we must remember that God is not respecter of persons. He wants the present day disciples to walk in the same authority and power as Jesus did when He was on the earth. To be a follower of Jesus we must walk as He did. Jesus said He loved God and kept His commands, therefore He abided in His love. As Jesus is so are we in this world. As Jesus is in love with the Father so can we be in love. If we walk in love as Jesus did with the Father there will be nothing that we can not do.

As we said before Jesus moved in authority and power because of three things:

1. Jesus was anointed with the Holy Ghost.

2. Jesus was anointed with power.

3. God was with Him (abiding relationship with God)

If we apply these three principles to our lives we will move in authority and power also. The first is receiving the baptism of the Holy Spirit. Receiving the Holy Spirit is God in us. It is a gift that is manifested by speaking in tongues. Some may look at speaking in tongues as useless; however, if that is their attitude they do not understand the significance of the gift. When we speak in tongues it is the language of the kingdom of God. Every kingdom has its own official language. It is the language God likes to hear from us. In Romans 8:26, it says," the Spirit makes intercession for us according to the will of God." This means the Spirit is praying for us according to the Fathers will. In Jude 20, we are exhorted to build up our faith by praying in the Spirit. Not only does it build up our faith but the Spirit causes us to stay in the love of God. It causes us to stay in the presence of God. By the Spirit, God is able to keep us from falling and bring us faultless in the presence with exceeding joy. Jude 20-25 says:

20.

But ye, beloved, building up yourselves on your most holy faith, praying in the Holy Ghost,

21.

Keep yourselves in the love of God, looking for the mercy of our Lord Jesus Christ unto eternal life.

22. *And of some have compassion, making a difference:*

23.

And others save with fear, pulling them out of the fire; hating even the garment spotted by the flesh.

24. *Now unto Him that is able to keep you from falling, And to present you faultless before the presence of His glory with exceeding joy,*

25.

To the only wise God our Savior, be glory and majesty, dominion and power, both now and ever. Amen.

In Luke 4:1 & 14, we see that when Jesus received the baptism of the Holy Ghost He went into the wilderness. The baptism of the Spirit allows us to encounter and be victorious over the enemy. The Spirit is able to keep us from falling as we saw in Jude. When Jesus comes out the wilderness it says He was full of the power of God. He was anointed with power. Jesus then goes to the synagogue and read the following; Luke 4:18 says:

*The Spirit of the Lord is upon me, because He hath **anointed** me to **preach** the gospel to the poor; He hath sent me to **heal** the broken-hearted, to **preach deliverance** to the captives,* *and **recovering sight** to the blind, to **set at liberty** them that are bruised.*

First of all Jesus says He was anointed. To be anointed means that God has imparted or empowered you to do a certain task. The Scripture says Jesus was anointed with the Holy Ghost or in other words it was imparted to Him. In Luke, Jesus says the Spirit of God is upon me because He has anointed me. I believe Jesus came into glory after the wilderness experience because He says the Spirit is upon Him. Jesus always made the distinction about God being in Him, which was the baptism of the Holy Spirit, and He being in God which is receiving the glory of God. Coming into glory is an individual coming into God, or coming into His presence. In John 17:22, Jesus says He has given us His glory to be perfect in one with Him. This is Jesus in us and we in Him. I believe that it was at this point Jesus knew the Father was with Him. We know He was submitted to God, because He says He kept the Fathers commands. This is walking in authority and power.

Jesus says the Spirit is upon me because He has been anointed to preach, heal, deliver etc. In other words he has been anointed with power to do these tasks. From these scriptures we see Jesus was anointed with the Holy Ghost and power. We also see God was with Him because He says the Spirit of God was upon Him, not just in Him.

The question now becomes how do we come to the point where we are anointed with the Holy Ghost, power and God is with us? For years I sought after the power of God and I sought to be in His presence. Sometimes I felt it had to be one or the other. I did not want God to think I just wanted His power to minister so I could look good. He knew my heart, and many times my motives were not right. What I have found is that we do not have to make a choice. He wants us to come into His fullness. He wants us to have His presence and move in His power. It is part of our destiny. I know I had received the anointing to heal. I received prophetic words about this ministry and I even had visions about it. I would see God heal in my life, and see God heal others in the visions. However, I was not getting the results that I knew God wanted. I had to ask the question why people were not healed in certain situations. The answer I received from God was that I can not heal anybody. Did not Jesus say of Himself, He could not do anything? We must also come into this realization. During this time the Lord also had me stay in John 15 and study it. The Lord spoke the following to me, "Have you ever seen a tree heal anybody?"

John 15: 1-17 says that we are the branches and Jesus is the vine. We are part of a tree and the Father is the husbandman or farmer. The fruit or the gifting given us comes off the branch. The fruit is the gifting or the anointing we have been given. These anointings are cultivated by being in Jesus or staying in His presence. If we look at how Jesus ministered He knew He could do nothing of Himself. He had the anointing but to do ministry He made the choice to seek the Father's will, so He could bring the Father glory. His first ministry was to the Father. Jesus said that it was the Father that was doing the work. Our gifts are developed in the presence of Jesus. Our first ministry is to the farmer or husbandman, Song of Solomon 4:16 and 5:1 shows this:

4:16.

Awake, O north wind; and come, thou south; blow upon my garden, that the spices thereof may flow out. Let my beloved come into his garden, and eat his pleasant fruits.

5:1.

I am come into my garden, my sister, my spouse: I have gathered my myrrh with my spice; I have eaten my honeycomb with my honey; I have drunk my wine with my milk: eat, O friends; drink, yea drink abundantly, O beloved.

He comes to His garden and is ministered to, he then calls in His friends to partake of the fruit. This goes with Psalms 29:2-3:

2.

Give unto the Lord the glory due unto his name; Worship the Lord in the beauty of holiness,

3.

The voice of the Lord is upon the waters: The God of glory thundereth: the Lord is upon many waters,

When the fruit is developed in us we must allow the Father to be ministered to first. We give Him glory by worship and praise. Jesus says in John 15:8,"Herein is the Father glorified, that you bear much fruit." In John 15:7, Jesus talks about abiding in Him and His words abiding in us and we asking what we will. We give Him glory by worshipping Him in the beauty of holiness (Psalm 29:2). It is then that the words or the voice of God that is in us is released. The scripture says that out of our bellies will flow rivers of living water. This is talking about the baptism of the Holy Spirit (John 7:38-39). The voice of God is on these waters. This is why praying in the Spirit or speaking in tongues is important because it is the releasing of the word or voice of God in us. Praying in the Spirit builds faith because faith says He is with me. This is why that if I have faith as a grain of mustard seed, I can say or release His voice or word that is in me, and the mountain I am praying about has to move. So God is not only glorified in the producing of fruit, but He is glorified by worship. He is glorified by our focus and love being on Him. The fruit is a product of the worship. This is why faith works by love (Galatians 5:6).

When God is ministered to then He invites His friends into the garden and releases His voice. The voice of the Lord is upon many waters. His voice is released on the rivers that flow out of our bellies. It is the Father's choice to do with the fruit as He wishes. In the case of healing, the Father, as it were, takes a grape of healing that comes off our branch and applies it to the person to get well. When God does the work, it is done. In preaching, God takes the seeds from the apple that comes from us and plants them in the right soil. In the parable about the seed going to the good soil, we see several things. The husbandman or farmer, He is the one who cultivates the plant and applies the seed. If we apply the seed it will almost always go to the wrong place.

John in Revelations 22:1-5, saw the throne of God and out of it came rivers of living water. On each side there was the tree of life in the midst of it. Psalms 1:3 says we are trees of life when we make God our delight. If we are not nourished by staying before the throne then we cannot have several kinds of fruit, or gifts, and there will not be healing in our leaves. Therefore, we glorify Him by delighting in Him.

Our authority and power comes from the Father. He is authority and power. He comes to us by manifesting His glory; the scripture says He comes with power (Isaiah 40:10). God will take our gifting, anointing or fruit and make it prosper. No matter how insignificant you think your gift is if you allow God to handle it He will make it great. If He could take a couple of fish and five loaves of bread from a little boy and feed a multitude, how much more can He multiply the anointing or gifting that is in us? Let's look at preaching again. We must allow God to direct our preaching, instead of us trying to develop an idea we must allow God to preach through us. I have known instances where God already prepared someone for the message He wanted you to speak. God will prepare the ground before you even speak a word. This is preaching according to His will. God breaks the hard ground in that individual to receive the specific word He has given you. I know of occasions where the Lord had our intercessors pray concerning a service and what He gave us to pray came about in the service. You might not see the result but God moved. Paul said it is for some to plant and for others to water. Sometimes the word you speak may not even be for that congregation, but you are speaking to the atmosphere. You are speaking to spirits that may have hold on a town. You may just be there to declare a word over an area. The area may be improvised and you are sent to speak prosperity. I was complaining once that I did not want to go to a certain country. The Lord said He may send me to an area just for one person. It is all about doing His will and bringing Him glory. What if Ananias did not speak the word to Paul while he was blind (Acts 9: 9-17)? We may not have received half of the New Testament. What if Ananias decided not to go to Paul because Paul helped kill fellow Christians? Could we blame him for not going? Ananias was obedient and look at the fruit God produced by one act of obedience. It is all about doing His will and bringing Him glory. He knows where the good ground is and He knows what seed needs to be planted where. Only His words bring Spirit and life. Jesus showed this in John 14.

John 14:10 says:

> *Believest thou not that I am in the Father, and the Father in me? The words that I speak unto you I speak not of myself: but the Father that dwelleth in me, He doeth the works.*

So how do we come into authority and power? To be like Jesus we must be anointed with the Holy Ghost, power and God must be with us. We receive the Holy Ghost by receiving the baptism of the Holy Spirit, speaking in tongues. To be anointed with power you must seek after it. There is a spirit of power that will come to you. Isaiah 11:2, talks about how Jesus received the spirit of might, or power. There is also a power that comes to us when He comes to us because we abide in His presence and He is in us. God takes us from glory to glory, and with each level of glory there is a corresponding level of power. Paul in I Corinthians 12: 27-31 says:

27.

Now ye are the body of Christ, and members in particular.

28.

And God hath set some in the church, first apostles, secondarily prophets, thirdly teachers, after that miracles, then gifts of healings, helps, governments, diversities of tongues.

29.

Are all apostles? are all prophets? Are all teachers? are all workers of miracles?

30.

Have all the gifts of healing? do all speak with tongues? do all interpret?

31.

But covet earnestly the best gifts.

In order to walk in ministries, gifts and power we must covet earnestly the best gifts, ministries and power. Sometimes we cannot heal because we were not anointed with the power to do it. There are many times when individuals in the church limit their potential. They may say someone was called to preach, but they have a desire for another ministry. I say seek God for the ministry and I know He will allow you to move in it. Paul says covet earnestly the best gifts. Do not let man or fear keep you from the best things God has to offer. God asked Solomon what did He want and God gave him the wisdom he asked the Lord for in prayer. God still asks what do we want. Which ministry, giftings or power do you want to move in? Do not let man hinder you from reaching your full potential. I know from experience that whatever ministry, gifting etc, that you seek, God will give it to you. It will not be for your sake but so He will be glorified.

How do we come to the point where we know He is with us? We see the answer in John 14:21-23:

21.

*He that hath my commandments, and keepth them, he it is that loveth me: and He that loveth me shall be loved of my Father, and I will love him, and will **manifest myself to him**.*

22.

Judas saith unto Him, not Iscariet, Lord, how is it that thou wilt manifest thyself unto us, and not the world?

23.

*Jesus answered and said unto him, if a man love me, he will keep my word: and my Father will love him, and we will come unto him, and make **our abode with him**.*

When God makes His abode with us we know He is with us. When we know He is with us that is faith. Our faith focus is not on what we want done but it is on the fact that He is with me. When we have this faith even as a grain of mustard seed we can speak to whatever mountain is in our lives and they will move.

Authority is also a result of knowing He is with us. James says draw near to God and He will draw near to us, and if we submit to God the devil will flee from us. This means that when I come under God's authority, I have authority. The centurion said because he was under authority he had authority to command. Jesus said the centurion had great faith. When I come under His authority I also have authority. We have the authority of God because we are heirs of God and joint-heirs with Jesus.

Because of the cross we have the ingredients to walk in authority and power. Daniel was correct that the saints of the Most High will inherit the kingdom and dominion. The power and authority of God belongs to the church of the living God. We do not have any excuse, because if we abide in Him and His words abide in us we will ask what we will and it will be done. As a branch on a tree we can do nothing, but with Jesus who is the vine and the Father who is the husbandman, we can do all things. This is our first point of confidence.

Chapter 6

USING HIS NAME

Our next point of confidence in prayer is using the name of Jesus. Once we realize that we can do nothing outside of abiding in Him, then we will see the release of authority and power in our lives. It is in the place of being a true worshipper that we will see people saved, healed and delivered. God seeks after the true worshipper, because the true worshipper seeks the Father's will, and looks to bring Him glory. Bringing him glory must become our motivation.

It is in the place of oneness with Jesus that I have a right to use His name. When we use His name what we are saying is that He is here to heal or do whatever we are praying about. The bible says in Philippians that Jesus was given a name above every name. Many times the critics of Jesus would ask Him by what name did He do His works, or by what authority. Several years ago God showed me how using the name of Jesus was a key that opened the door to the power of God. The question then becomes if I use the name of Jesus in prayer why doesn't it happen? When Jesus talked about praying in His name I believe He wanted us to go beyond just speaking His name verbally, but come into a place in God where He gives us His name or His authority to use.

John 14: 10-14 &20 says:

10.

*Believest thou not **that I am in the Father, and the Father, and the Father in me?** The words that I speak unto you I speak not of myself: but the Father that dwelleth in me, He doth the works.*

11.

Believe me that I am in the Father, and the Father in me; or else believe me for the very works sake.

12.

*Verily, verily, I say unto you, He that believeth on me, the **works that I do shall He do also**; and **greater works** than these shall he do; because I go unto my Father.*

13.

And whatsoever ye shall ask in my name, that will I do, that the Father may be glorified in the Son.

14.

If ye ask anything in my name, I will do it.

20.

At that day ye shall know that I am in my Father, and ye in me, and I in you.

There are four factors that we see from these scriptures that will show us to how we come to use the name of Jesus and the results of using His name.

1. Jesus and the Father are one; from this relationship Jesus had power and authority. We are also called to oneness.

2. We can do the works of Jesus, which is to abide with the Father.

3. Because I am sanctified, He gives me His name and I ask for what I will.

4. We know Jesus will answer us so the Father will be glorified.

The first factor was that Jesus and the Father are one. It was from this relationship that Jesus had the right to use the name or authority of God. Philippians 2:5-10 shows us that Jesus was obedient to death. Jesus says in John 15:10 that He kept the Father's commands and abided in His love. The result of Jesus abiding was that He was given a name above all names. Jesus said all power and authority was His.

The second factor says we can do His works. Many times when people look at these passages they think of the gifting and power of Jesus. But the main work Jesus did was to abide in love by keeping the Fathers commands. When we do these works we are one with Jesus we have a right to use His name.

We showed earlier that we are in Jesus by God, who is made to us wisdom, righteousness, sanctification and redemption. Because of the cross we have a right to His name or authority.

II Chronicles 7:15 - 16 says:

> *15.*
>
> *Now mine eyes shall be open, and mine ears attent unto the prayer that is made in this place.*
>
> *16.*
>
> *For now have I chosen and **sanctified** this house, that **my name** may be there forever: and mine eyes and heart shall be there perpetually.*

This was the result of the children of Israel humbling themselves, praying, seeking His face and turning from their wicked ways. Remember Jesus humbled Himself by being obedient. When God saw the children of Israel humble themselves He gave them His name or authority. The result of having His name is in verse 15 where God says that He will answer their prayer. So we see that sanctification causes us to be one and the results of this are that we can use His name and God will answer our prayer. This was the third factor that we saw from the passage in John 14. Using His name is the key that opens the door to the power of God.

John in Revelations 22:1-2, talks about seeing the rivers of living water coming out of the throne of God. On every side were the trees of life, which bore fruit. Psalms 1:2-3, says we will be as trees of life when we delight in the Lord. Those that delight in the Lord love Him. Jesus said those that love Him abide in Him and keep His commands. So if one abides they are like a tree of life, because they are before the throne of God. The promise we have for abiding is in Revelations 22:3-4.

Revelations 22:3-4 says:

3.

*And there shall be no curse: but the throne of God and of the
Lamb shall be in it; and His servants shall serve Him:*

4.

*And they shall see His face; and **His name shall be on their
foreheads**.*

We see this again in Revelations 3: 12, which says:

12.

*Him that overcometh will I make a pillar in temple of my God,
and he shall go no more out: and I will write upon Him the
name of my God, and the name of the city of my God,
which is the new Jerusulem, which cometh down out of heaven
from my God: and I will write upon him my **new name**.*

The one that overcomes will not leave the temple or will abide in Him.
The result of this is receiving the name or authority of God. When I
use that name in prayer, I am saying that Jesus is present to heal or do
whatever needs to be done.

In Mark 16:17-20, Jesus says that these signs will follow them that
believe, in my name they will deliver, heal etc. When you believe you
know you are righteous, sanctified and redeemed. The result of this is
that your one with God and given His name. The result of this is that
Jesus will answer. In Mark 16:20 it says, they went forth, and preached

everywhere, **the Lord** working with them, and confirming the word with signs following. This was after the cross, which shows the Jesus was with those that prayed in His name.

The fourth factor in John 14: 10-14, is the reason we use His name. Jesus says that He will answer when we pray in His name so that the Father is glorified. To bring God glory or to glorify God means to cause a shout or cause praise to happen in heaven because of the greatness of God. Luke 15:7 says; there is joy in heaven over one sinner that repents. This means that every time the enemy is defeated in someone's life the angels in heaven rejoice.

When we stand in the place of using His name with the motive of bringing Him glory, we will see the voice of God released in a situation. We will then see our prayers answered.

Psalms 29: 1-4 says:

1.

*Give unto the Lord, O ye mighty, give unto the **glory** and strength.*

2.

*Give unto the Lord the **glory** due His name; worship the Lord in the **beauty of holiness**.*

3.

*The **voice of the Lord** is upon the water: the God of glory thundereth: the Lord is upon many waters.*

4.

> *The voice of the Lord is powerful; the voice of the Lord is full of majesty.*

When His voice is released He will bring the answer to our prayer. Using His name is the key to release or open the door to the power of God. When God speaks or sends His word He will do it. The centurion in Matthew 8: 8-10, told Jesus to speak the word only and his servant would be healed. The centurion understood the authority that Jesus had and that Jesus only needed to speak the word for the situation to be resolved. We see another example of this in Exodus 34. Exodus 34:5-10 says:

5.

> *And the Lord descended in the cloud, and stood with him there, and **proclaimed the name of the Lord**.*

6.

> *And the Lord passed by before him, and proclaimed, The Lord, The Lord God, merciful and gracious, longsuffering, and abundant in goodness and truth,*

7.

> *Keeping mercy for thousands, forgiving iniquity and transgression and sin, and that will by no means clear the guilty; visiting the iniquity of the fathers upon the children, and upon the children's children, unto the third and to the fourth generation.*

8.

And Moses made haste, and bowed his head toward the earth, and worshipped.

9.

*And he said, If now I have found grace in thy sight, O Lord, let my Lord, **I pray thee**, go among us; for it is a stiff necked; and pardon our iniquity and our sin, and take us for thine inheritance.*

10.

*And he said, Behold I make a covenant; before all thy people I will do marvels, such as have not been done in all the earth, nor in any nation: and all the people among which thou art shall **see the work of the Lord**: for it is a terrible thing that I will do with thee.*

We see Moses in the place of His presence where God comes and proclaims His name. God proclaimed His name then Moses knew how to pray. When Moses prayed he knew God would forgive the iniquity of the people, because of the proclamation of the Lord. In verse 10, God answers by making covenant with the people and promises to work with them.

When God proclaims His name to us He is showing us how He wants to move. When we pray in His name, we have a promise that He will move according to His name. When He proclaims His name He is giving us authority to pray according to that name. We know

God will answer, because Jesus promises He will move so the Father is glorified.

When we realize we are sanctified and redeemed we will realize we are heirs of God and joint-heirs of Jesus. This is when we will realize we have a right to use His name because we are part of the family of God. When you are part of a family you have a right to use the family name. When we move as Jesus did looking for the will of the Father and looking to glorify God, when we use Jesus name, Jesus promises to answer. He will answer for one reason and one reason only: It is so the Father will be glorified (John 14).

God wants us to be a confident people in prayer. First He causes us to be confident by making us righteous, sanctified and redeemed. Through these together we can come to the throne boldly.

Hebrews 4:16 says:

> *Let us therefore come boldly unto the throne of grace, that we may obtain mercy, and find grace to help in a time of need.*

The name of Jesus is also given to us to use so that we can pray in confidence, knowing God will answer. Peter called this faith in His name, Acts 3:16:

> *And his name through faith in his name hath made this man strong, whom ye see and know: yea, the faith which is by him hath given him perfect soundness in the presence of you all.*

Using the name of Jesus is based on a promise.

John 14:13 says:

> *And whatever ye **ask in my name**, that will I do, that the Father may be glorified in the Son.*

This is a point of confidence that we can stand on so that we know He will answer.

Chapter 7

WHEN THE RIGHTEOUS PRAY

The first two points of confidence in our prayer lives are: Abiding with Him so that we know He is with us, and using His name. The third point of confidence is because we are righteous God will answer our prayer.

James 5:16 says:

> *Confess your faults one to another that ye may be healed. The effectual fervent prayer of the righteous man availeth much.*

I Peter 3:12 says:

> *God's eyes are on the righteous, and His ears are open unto their prayer: but the face of the Lord is against them that do evil.*

When we walk in our righteousness that means there is no separation between God and us. Our third point of confidence is that because we are righteous His eyes are on us and His ears are open to our prayers. The Lord gave me a vision on how He can see and be with all those that seek Him. It was as a sea with many faces in it, and He could see all those that sought Him.

Our prayers being answered have nothing to do with us and our ability. We are righteous because of the blood of Jesus, and He answers us so the Father will be glorified. This is why we can stand in confidence and know whatever we pray He will do. In fact Jesus tells the disciples six times about praying and He will answer.

1. *John 14: 13 – and whatever ye shall **ask** in my name, that will I do, that the Father may be glorified in the Son.*
2. *John 14:14 – If ye shall ask anything in my name, I will do it.*
3. *John 15:7 – If ye abide in me, and my words abide in you, ye shall ask what ye will, and it shall be done unto you.*
4. *John 15:16 – Whatsoever ye shall ask of the Father in my name, He may give it you.*
5. *John 16:23 – Whatsoever ye shall ask the Father in my name, He will give it you.*
6. *John 16:24 – Hitherto have ye asked nothing in my name; ask, and ye shall receive, that your joy may be full.*

In order for these scriptures to be real for us we must walk in righteousness. I believe Jesus was trying to get the message across to us that whatever we pray in His name He will do it. When we move in this type of confidence there will be nothing impossible for us. Let's look at what happens when the righteous pray.

Examples of when the righteous pray

When we look at how the righteous are to pray we can look at Jesus for one of our examples. As we have seen in previous chapters the keys to Jesus' ministry was that He looked to do the Father's will and to glorify the Father. It was because of this God answered Him.

Let's look at Moses for another example.

Numbers 20: 6-12 says:

6.

> And Moses and Aaron went from the presence of the assembly unto the door of the tabernacle of the congregation, and they fell upon their faces: and the **glory of the Lord appeared unto them**.

7.

> And the Lord spake unto Moses, saying,

8.

> Take the rod, and gather thou the assembly together, thou and Aaron thy brother, and **speak ye unto the rock** before their eyes: and it shall give forth his water, and thou shalt bring forth to them water out of the rock: so thou shalt give the congregation and their beasts drink.

9.

> And Moses took the rod from before the Lord, as He commanded him.

10.

*And Moses and Aaron gathered the congregation together before the rock, and he said unto them, Hear now, ye rebels;must **we** fetch you water out of this rock?*

11.

*And Moses lifted up his hand, **and with his rod he smote the rock twice**: and the water came out abundantly, and the congregation drank, and their beasts also.*

12.

*And the Lord spoke unto Moses and Aaron, Because ye believed me not, to **sanctify me** in the eyes of the children of Israel, therefore ye shall not bring this congregation into the land which I have given them.*

We see in this situation that the people were not happy because there was no water. They were so discouraged that they wanted to turn from what God told them. Moses and Aaron go and seek God and verse 6 says that the glory of God came. This shows that God was with them because they were in glory. They were in the presence of God. Moses told God about the situation of no water and God told Moses His will or strategy for the situation. God tells Moses to speak to the rock and water would come forth. In the past God had Moses hit a rock to bring forth water (Exodus 17:6). So Moses had the ingredients to move in authority and power. Moses and Aaron knew God was with them, they knew His will for the situation, and they were anointed with authority and power. However, they failed in this situation. As we continue to look at this story we see that when Moses dealt with the people he was angry and hit the rock, instead of speaking to it. The water came because of the anointing on Moses, but God was not happy. In Numbers 20:12, God tells Moses that he did not believe Him, to sanctify Him in the eyes of the people. In other words Moses did not give God glory in this situation by being obedient. In verse 10, Moses says must **we** fetch the water out of the rock? Moses was confident in his past anointing; however, God was trying to take him to a new level of power by just speaking the word. Jesus was successful in ministry because He always looks to glorify the Father. By glorifying Him we produce fruit. The seed of His word is put into people's hearts and they come to know that God is real and that He loves them. When we try to get glory then the work God wants to do in people's hearts cannot be done. In this situation God moved because Moses was righteous; however, all that God wanted accomplished in people's hearts through Moses was not done. In I Corinthians 2: 4-5, Paul says he used the demonstration of the Spirit and of power so that the people's faith would not stand on man's wisdom but in the power of God. God wanted the people's eyes on Him and not Moses.

The Prayer of Elijah

In James 5:15-18, it says that the prayer of the righteous avails much. James then uses Elijah as an example of this. We can assume Elijah was righteous but how did the rain stop and come by his word? What was the key to Elijah's successes?

We are introduced to Elijah in I Kings 17: 1. In this verse Elijah says:

> *As the Lord God of Israel liveth, before whom I stand, there shall not be dew nor rain these years, but according to my word.*

You would think from this passage that Elijah just went and spoke these words to Ahab. However, we see in I Kings 18:1 that Elijah, like Jesus and Moses waited for the word of God to come before they moved.

I Kings 18:1 says:

> *And it came to pass after many days that **the word of the Lord** came to Elijah in the third year, saying Go, show thyself unto Ahab; and **I will send rain upon the earth.***

Galatians 3:5-6 says:

> 5.
>
> *He therefore that **ministereth to you the spirit, and works miracles** among you doeth he it by the works of the law, or by the **hearing of faith?***

> 6.
>
> *Even as Abraham believed God, and it was accounted to him for **righteousness.***

James said the effectual fervent prayer of the righteous avails much. Why? Because when one walks in righteousness there is no separation between you and God. You are then in the place to hear God to know how to pray in the situation to see the miracle come to pass. Righteousness and faith are as a cord wrapped together that leads us to God and to answered prayer.

After Elijah sees Ahab he goes to the mountain and prays. He prays until the rain comes. He had confidence that God would answer because God showed Elijah what He was ready to do. The interesting thing was God waited to move until He heard Elijah pray concerning the situation.

The Lord gave me a vision of how He was bringing the church into different types of prayer. As we grow in Christ, God takes us from faith to faith. As He does this our prayer life must move with our faith. There is the prophetic prayer, and apostolic prayer that God is bringing the church into. Elijah prayed a prophetic prayer. This is a prayer where you receive the word and you pray the will of God. The apostle takes the prophetic word and establishes the purposes of God. The apostle with the Lords help puts the wheels on the work that God has given them. An example of apostolic prayer is when Abraham knows that God wants to destroy Sodom. Abraham prays for the mercy of God for the people and he changes God's mind.

Another example is Daniel. Daniel sees that Jeremiahs prophecy that the exile was to end after 70 years. Daniel fasts and prays for the word to come to pass. His praying released angels to move on his behalf. The children of Israel were taken captive in 605 B.C. and the first exiles to return to Judah were in 538 B.C, which was a total of 67 years. Jesus is the chief apostle who ever makes intercession for us at the throne of God. In Philippians 2, it talks about placing the things of others before yourself, and to let this mind be in you that was in Christ Jesus. What was His mind? It was to lay His life down for us. We can do this also through intercession for others. This is knowing the will of God for individuals and praying that God bring it to pass. What a powerful calling that is. We can be like Daniel and change the history of a people.

The righteous are those who are before the face of God.

I Peter 3:12:

> *For the eyes of the Lord are over the righteous, and his ears are open unto their prayers: but the face of the Lord is against them that do evil.*

The righteous have God's face when they have His eyes and ears on them. In 2 Chronicles 7:14-16, those that seek His face are promised His eyes, ears and heart. What a glorious inheritance that the righteous have. When we have His face, nothing is impossible for us.

Chapter 8

WATCH AND PRAY

In the book of Mark, before Jesus is taken away one of the last lessons He teaches His disciples on prayer is to watch and pray.

Mark 14: 38 says:

> *Watch ye and pray, lest ye enter into temptation. The spirit is truly is ready, but the flesh is weak.*

There were many things Jesus could have told the disciples before dying on the cross, however He tells them to watch and pray. I always wondered what watching meant in the word. The Lord then showed me Habakkuk 2:1-4.

Habakkuk 2: 1-4 says:

> *1.*

> *I will stand upon my watch, and set me upon the tower, and will **watch to see** what He will **say** unto me, and I will answer when I am reproved.*

2.

And the Lord answered me, and said, write the vision, and make it plain upon tables, that he may run the readeth it.

3.

For the vision is yet for an appointed time, but at the end it shall speak, and not lie: though it tarry, wait for it; because it will surely come, it will not tarry.

4.

*Behold his soul which is lifted up is not upright in him: but **the just live by His faith**.*

Habakkuk says, "He will watch to see what the Lord will say to him." He was waiting for the direction of God before he moved. As we have seen this has been the pattern of those that walk in the way of power.

An important point in this passage is that he says he will watch to see what God will say. God does not just want to speak to us but He wants us to be able to see in the spirit realm.

One of the reasons we are given the Holy Spirit is so we can see in the spirit realm.

Acts 2: 17-20 says:

17.

And it shall come to pass in the last days, saith God, I will pour out of my Spirit upon all flesh: and your sons and your *daughters shall prophesy, and your young men shall **see visions**, and your old men shall **dream dreams**:*

18.

And on my servants and on my handmaidens I will pour out in those days of my Spirit; and they shall prophesy:

19.

*And **I will show wonders** in heaven above, and signs in the earth beneath; blood, and fire, and vapor of smoke:*

20.

The sun shall be turned into darkness, and the moon into blood, before that great and notable day of the Lord come:

We see from this Scripture that the young men are to see visions and the old men are to dream dreams. The Holy Spirit is given not so we can just hear Him, but He is given so that we can see in the spirit realm.

The reason this is important is because if we are following Jesus' example, then we must move in ministry as He did. Jesus said that He only does what He **sees** the Father do (John 5:19). Watching involves seeing what the Lord will say or do so we know how to move in a situation. This gives God glory because we are humbly coming before Him looking for His direction. David said he never saw the righteous forsaken or his seed begging bread. This is not just in the natural realm. David never saw the righteous forsaken when they needed direction from the Father. Whenever David needed direction God gave it to him. David did not go to war unless he knew God was going with him.

When Jesus said to the disciples watch and pray He was telling the disciples to be like Habakkuk. They were to see what the Lord was saying, then pray according to His will. This is when the Lord will move on our behalf so the Father will be glorified in the Son.

We are all called to be watchmen not just pastors or intercessors. Wherever you are at in life you are to stand in authority and power and you are to watch. It may be for your family, job or your church. You may be the only one saved in your family and you are to be the watchman over your family. You must seek God for His vision or strategy for your family. Then you are to pray that God bring it to pass. You may be a watchman for your church or your community. You do not have to be in leadership but seek God for the vision for your church or community and then pray until God brings the vision to pass.

Jude 1: 20-21, and Philippians 3:20, shows us how we can come into a place of watching.

Jude 1:20-21 says:

20.

But ye beloved, building up yourselves on you most holy faith, ***praying in the Holy Spirit,***

21.

Keep yourselves in the love of God, looking *for the mercy of our Lord Jesus Christ unto eternal life.*

Philippians 3:20 says:

> *For our conversation is in heaven; from whence also we **look** for the Saviour, the Lord Jesus Christ.*

As we saw in Acts the baptism of the Holy Spirit brings us to a place of seeing in the spirit. The Scriptures in Jude and Philippians show that praying in the Holy Spirit does several things as;

1. It builds up our faith.
2. It keeps us in the love of God. This is the abiding relationship.
3. In the place of abiding we can look for the Lord Jesus.

This is important because it is key to our ministering. Jesus said He only did what He saw the Father do. As we stay in love we will be able to see what Jesus is doing and act accordingly. In John 17:24, Jesus prays that we be where He is and that is in Him, and He in us, that we behold or see His glory. Seeing His glory is watching. How does God do this? Ephesians 3:17 gives us the answer:

> ***That Christ may dwell in your hearts by faith;*** that ye, being rooted and grounded in love,

This is beyond the baptism of the Spirit. This is when God opens a door in you where you experience Christ in you. This is when you are where He is and you can behold His glory. This is what Jesus means in John 14:23, when He says He and the Father will come and make their abode in you. When you realize this you can behold the Lord on a daily basis. I heard a preacher named David Herzog preach, "That there is no time or distance in the glory realm." The Father and Jesus are in heaven, but by the Spirit we can experience them in us. This is watching in the spirit realm.

> *But he that is joined unto the Lord is one spirit. I Corinthians 6:17*

Remember that Daniel said, "The saints of the Most High will inherit glory, the kingdom and dominion." Moving in dominion will happen when we realize we have authority and power. The extent we know this will determine how effective we are in watching and praying.

Chapter 9

HEALING KEYS

Several years ago the Lord dealt with us on how He was bringing healings and miracles to State College PA. Part of our intercession in our church, Unity Church of Jesus Christ, at that time was to pray that God bring this to pass. After several years, my pastor, Harold McKenzie, introduced me to another pastor in our city, David Janssen. He is the pastor of the Christian and Missionary Alliance Church in our town. I came to find out that the Lord had been giving them the same vision and they had been doing healing services on Sunday nights. They had been seeing the Lord cause cancers disappear. They have had 10-17 cases where the doctor saw a tumor and the patient would go back and it would be gone. They were very gracious, and allowed me to work with their healing team on Sunday nights. We have also taken what we learned at Pastor Janssen's church and used it in our own. Since that time we have seen the Lord do many marvelous things. Cancers, vision problems, and people on death beds have been healed. They look at it as a community healing service. There are several healing keys that I have learned since working with this group.

They are as follows:

1. The Lord told me that the main reason He heals is because He loves us.

2. When praying for someone, keep it simple. The Lord told me all you have to say is, "Be healed in the name of Jesus." The prayer of faith will save the sick, and the Lord will raise them up (James 5:15).

3. Use discernment; wait for the Lord to show you how to move.

4. It is always His will to heal someone. In a vision I saw someone praying if it be thy will, and I saw the Lord stand and turn His back weeping. He said it is always His will to heal. Now there have been times when the Lord told me it was that person's time to die, and you need to be sensitive to the person and the family. However, there are also some instances when God may say it is time to die, but as in the case of Hezekiah, the friend of God was able to change God's mind. Some will say why didn't God heal or why did someone die. Smith Wigglesworth said, "If I pray for a 100 people and they die, I will still believe that God is a healer." That has to be our attitude.

5. When Jesus was whipped before going to the cross, the Lord said that He looked at that as the price being paid for healing of generations to come. We can not earn a healing, the price was already paid.

6. God will answer according to where the person is at. If they believe God will heal through doctors, I have seen God move that way. The woman with the issue of blood said if I can but touch the hem of His garment I will be healed and she was (Matthew 9:21). The centurion said speak the word only, and his servant will be healed. Jesus moved because of their faith (Luke: 7:1-8).

7. Believe. These signs will follow those that believe (Mark 16:17). I found that the people on the healing teams do not have to know the in's and out's of healing all they need to do is believe Jesus is the healer.

8. Worship is key in releasing the hand of God in a service. As we minister to Him, His voice is released (Psalm 29).

9. Those that are prayed for need to stay in praise, and if the enemy or pain comes back rebuke it with your mouth. I saw a spirit of sickness try to come on me. I rebuked it and after awhile it left. We must fight until we get a breakthrough. Do not give up just because the enemy did not move after one prayer.

10. Before you get off your medication, go back to the doctor for confirmation of your healing, unless the Lord leads you to stop.

11. Do not let doctors steal your faith. You will know you are healed before the doctor knows, because many times they cannot see what God has done in the spirit.

12. If fear comes rebuke it.

13. Sometimes things in your family line need to be broken, as heart disease, cancer and other diseases.

14. Discern if the sickness is due to a spirit of infirmity (Luke 13:11). If it is rebuke it.

15. Discern if there is any witchcraft involved. I knew a woman who was sick and someone had given her a crystal which was supposed to bring about positive energy.

    This is witchcraft because you are looking to another spiritual source other than God for your peace, healing, and well being. Once this woman got rid of the crystal she was doing better.

16. Forgiveness is a major key for your healing. If we do not forgive we open the door to the enemy to come in and make us sick.

17. Step in faith once you're prayed for by an individual. An example would be to move the part of your body that you could not move before or was in pain.

18. Release the past. There are times the Lord will heal past hurts so you can receive your healing today.

19. Rebuke stress, and depression. Declare peace and refreshing.

20. Corporate prayer. I have seen when everyone got together to pray for someone's healing and that person was healed.

21. Singing over the sick. There have been times the Lord had us sing over someone and they were healed.

22. Prophesying over the sick. There are times when God will speak a prophetic word and the person is healed.

23. Be sensitive and gentle with God's people.

24. Let the sick sit down if they are in a church service and not feeling well.

25. Anoint with oil. James 5:14 says:

> *Is any sick among you? let him call for the elders of the church; and let them pray over him, **anointing him with oil** in the name of the Lord:*

The oil represents the Holy Spirit, and what you are saying is that the Lord is here to heal you, by faith.

26. To receive your healing you must realize that Jesus is there to heal you. Jesus is the healer. Where two or three are gathered together in my name, there am I in the midst of them (Matthew 18:20).

These are some of the keys God has given us since working with the healing team at CMA. I pray God will take you from glory to glory in your healing and miracle ministry also.

Chapter 10

ALL POWER AND AUTHORITY IS OURS

There had been a span of several years when I searched after the authority and power of God. While I was praying the Lord told me I just had to receive it. At that time I did not understand what the Lord meant. Then I was reading I Corinthians 1:24, which says, that Christ is the power and the wisdom of God. The Lord then had me read I Corinthians I: 29 – 30, which says:

29.

> *That no flesh should glory in His presence.*

30.

> *But of Him are ye in Christ Jesus, who of God is made unto us **wisdom**, and righteousness, and sanctification, and redemption.*

After reading these Scriptures together I realized that just as I receive His wisdom, righteousness, sanctification and redemption because of the cross, I can also receive His authority and power because of the cross. The word says He is wisdom in verse 24, then in verse 30 it says Jesus is made wisdom for us. Just as He is wisdom for us He is also power for us so that we have nothing to glory about in His presence.

Having power and authority has nothing to do with us. It is all about Jesus and Him being crucified. We have all authority and power because He has it all. Because I am seated in heavenly places in Christ Jesus, I have authority. The centurion said because he was under authority he had authority. When I yield to righteousness and abide I am in Him and under His authority. Therefore I have authority. Because I am in Christ, Jesus is also made power for me. He is the power of God.

The Lord showed me I could not receive the fact I had all power and authority because my heart was not right. I thought it was something I could gain so that I could be accepted by man. But God brought me full circle and showed me that as I receive Him, He will come with all authority and power. We do not have authority and power apart from Him.

When we know He is with us and therefore His power and authority is with us, we then have faith in His name or authority. In Acts 3, Peter and John heal a man that was lame. When the people saw this they wanted to exalt Peter and John.

Acts 3: 12, 16 & 4:10 says:

> *12.*
>
> *And when Peter saw it, he answered unto the people, Ye men of Israel, why marvel ye at this? or why look ye so earnestly on*

*us, as though by our own **power or holiness** we had made this man to walk?*

16.

*And **His name**, through **faith in His name**, hath made this man strong, whom ye see and know: yea, the **faith which is by Him** hath given him this perfect soundness in the presence of you all.*

4:10.

*Be it known unto you all, and to all the people of Israel, that **by the name of Jesus Christ of Nazareth**, whom ye crucified, whom God raised from the dead, **even by Him** doeth this man stand before you whole.*

Peter and John understood they did not have power in and of themselves. They said it was faith in His name or authority that made this man well. They had faith in the fact that God was with them, and when God is with us we know we have all power and authority. In Acts 4:10 we see this again, it was by the name of Jesus and it was by Him that the work was done. Faith says that He is, or that He is with us. Our faith focus is not the thing we want done, but it is in the fact that He is present with us. Jesus said if we have this type of faith even as the size of a mustard seed we can move mountains.

The way of power and authority is through Jesus Christ. He is the way, the truth and life. Jesus is the power and authority of God. When I know I have Him then I know I have the power and authority of God within me. The extent that He is present in my life is the extent of His power that will be released in my life. Moving in His power is not a mystery because the way has been made for the church through Jesus being crucified. We can move in the same authority and power Jesus did while He was on the earth. The word of God is true. We will do His works and greater because He has gone to the Father. As Jesus is so are we in this world (I John 4:17).

The key to the way to authority and power can be summed up in Isaiah 40:10, it says:

> *Behold, the Lord God will come with **power,** and His arm shall rule for Him: **behold, His reward is with Him, and His** work before Him.*

Jesus is the way to the authority and power of God. All we have to do is receive it.

> *God bless you and may you walk in His authority and power. The Lord said to me that we are on the precipice of a great healing movement. Are you ready? The mantra of the coming days will be "The Healing Jesus".*
>
> *Rick Rannie*

Pastor Rick Rannie is available for ministry at your church, or conferences. He can be contacted at the following address:

634 Southgate Dr
State College PA 16801

Telephone - 814 404 3065
Email – rannieglory@yahoo.com

CPSIA information can be obtained at www.ICGtesting.com
Printed in the USA
BVOW012327091211

278015BV00003B/83/P